NATURAL DISASTERS
MEETING THE CHALLENGE

WILDFIRE
READINESS

Kylie Burns
Crabtree Publishing Company
www.crabtreebooks.com

CRABTREE

PUBLISHING COMPANY

WWW.CRABTREEBOOKS.COM

Author: Kylie Burns

Series research and development:
Janine Deschenes, Reagan Miller

Editorial director: Kathy Middleton

Editors: Ellen Rodger, Melissa Boyce

Proofreader: Wendy Scavuzzo

Design and photo research:
Katherine Berti

Print and production coordinator:
Katherine Berti

Images:

Alamy Stock Photo: FORGET Patrick/
SAGAPHOTO.COM: p. 41 (bottom)
Associated Press: Andre Penner:
p. 4 (bottom)
© Copyright Triad National Security, LLC.
All Rights Reserved: p. 28 (inset, top)
EmiControls!: p. 39 (bottom left)
firemap.sdsc.edu—Screen Shot 2019-09-06
at 3.07.27 PM: p. 40 (inset)
Flickr
European Space Agency, contains
modified Copernicus Sentinel data
(2019), processed by ESA,CC BY-SA
3.0 IGO: p. 17 (bottom)
Dan Borsum, NOAA:NWS:WR:WFO,
Billings Montana: p. 16 (top)
NOAA Satellites: p. 16 (bottom)
Pavel Koubek, Icon Photography:
p. 17 (top)
Getty Images
Hindustan Times: p. 39 (top)
Justin Sullivan: p. 32–33 (bottom)
Istockphoto
Mimadeo: p. 31
sierrarat: p. 41 (top)
NASA: p. 24 (bottom)
Earth Observatory, Joshua Stevens,
using data provided by Matt Jolly,
USDA Forest Service: p. 6 (bottom)
GISS, Pechony: p. 25 (inset, bottom)

Jeff Schmaltz, LANCE:EOSDIS Rapid
Response: p. 4 (top)
Joshua Stevens: p. 18
METI:AIST:Japan Space Systems, and
U.S.:Japan ASTER Science Team: p. 20
NIST: Alex Maranghides: p. 11 (right)
Shutterstock
BrittanyNY: p. 11 (left)
Geartooth Productions: p. 43 (top)
J. Michael Jones: p. 30 (top)
Joseph Sohm: p. 29
Krista Kennell: p. 42
Mike Chapman: p. 38
mikeledray: p. 21 (top)
Robert Paul Van Beets: p. 30 (bottom)
The Canadian Press: Jonathan Hayward: p. 27
U.S. Navy: Deris Jeannette: p. 35 (bottom)
Wikimedia Commons
DarrenRD: p. 26 (bottom)
Eric Neitzel: p. 14
Fish and Wildlife Service Southeast
Region: p. 8
Maarten Visser: p. 23 (top)
Pacific Southwest Region 5: p. 37 (top)
U.S. Air Force: Chris Miller: p. 23 (bottom)
U.S. Army Corps of Engineers
Sacramento District: p. 35 (top)
U.S. Forest Service, Pacific Northwest
Region: p. 12
Wyoming National Guard Photo by
1st Lt. Christian Venhuizen: p. 36
All other images by Shutterstock

Library and Archives Canada Cataloguing in Publication

Title: Wildfire readiness / Kylie Burns.
Names: Burns, Kylie, author.
Description: Series statement: Natural disasters:
meeting the challenge | Includes bibliographical
references and index.
Identifiers: Canadiana (print) 20190134399 |
Canadiana (ebook) 20190134402 |
ISBN 9780778765257 (hardcover) |
ISBN 9780778765318 (softcover) |
ISBN 9781427123831 (HTML)
Subjects: LCSH: Wildfires—Juvenile literature. | LCSH:
Emergency management—Juvenile literature.
Classification: LCC SD421.23 .B87 2019 | DDC j634.9/618—dc23

Library of Congress Cataloging-in-Publication Data

Names: Burns, Kylie, author.
Title: Wildfire readiness / Kylie Burns.
Description: New York, New York : Crabtree Publishing Company,
[2020] | Series: Natural disasters: meeting the challenge |
Includes bibliographical references and index.
Identifiers: LCCN 2019026951 (print) | LCCN 2019026952 (ebook) |
ISBN 9780778765257 (hardcover) |
ISBN 9780778765318 (paperback) | ISBN 9781427123831 (ebook)
Subjects: LCSH: Wildfires--Juvenile literature. | Wildfires--Prevention
and control--Juvenile literature.
Classification: LCC SD421.23 .B87 2020 (print) | LCC SD421.23 (ebook) |
DDC 634.9/618--dc23
LC record available at https://lccn.loc.gov/2019026951
LC ebook record available at https://lccn.loc.gov/2019026952

Crabtree Publishing Company

www.crabtreebooks.com   1-800-387-7650

Printed in the U.S.A./102019/CG20190809

**Published
in Canada
Crabtree Publishing**
616 Welland Ave.
St. Catharines, Ontario
L2M 5V6

**Published in the
United States
Crabtree Publishing**
PMB 59051
350 Fifth Avenue, 59th Floor
New York, New York 10118

**Published in the
United Kingdom
Crabtree Publishing**
Maritime House
Basin Road North, Hove
BN41 1WR

**Published
in Australia
Crabtree Publishing**
Unit 3–5 Currumbin Court
Capalaba
QLD 4157

Contents

Wild Wildfires

Images such as this one captured by a NASA satellite show the vast size and spread of the 2003 Siberian Taiga Fires.

In the history of wildfires, the 2003 Siberian Taiga Fires in Russia, Northern China, and Mongolia burned more land than any other on record. The fires destroyed more than 47 million acres (19 million ha) of forest across Eurasia. The thick smoke could be seen on NASA satellite images from space.

Wildfires often burn in remote areas, but increasingly, they also affect nearby cities and towns where people live. These fiery forces of nature have a negative impact on the social, political, and environmental well-being of communities around the world.

Smoke

Lake Baikal

*Fires in the Amazon rain forest in 2019 were said to have been deliberately set by ranchers and farmers seeking to claim land. More than 2.5 million square miles (6.5 million sq km) burned. The rain forest has a dry season when fires naturally occur, but fires **ignited** by humans claim more territory.*

What Is a Wildfire?

A wildfire is a fire that is burning out of control in a forest, prairie, or **rural** area. Also called wildland fires, forest fires, or bush fires, they destroy large areas of land. As cities and towns expand onto the fringes of wildlands, wildfires are having an impact on **urban** areas. Wildfires have the potential to become deadly catastrophes as they destroy buildings and homes in developed areas, and jump across roads.

A large wildfire affects the environment in various ways, including animal habitat destruction, and air pollution which can lead to long-term air quality concerns. Some wildfires are started naturally by a random lightning strike, but statistics show that four out of five wildfires are started by people. Sometimes, they are caused by a campfire that hasn't been extinguished properly, and occasionally they are started by **arson**.

Wild, but Natural

A wildfire is a natural event, because it occurs as a result of certain conditions in nature. A wildfire becomes a natural disaster when it affects life on the planet. Even though these disasters have terrible effects on people and the environment throughout the world, there are many things that can be learned through studying and understanding natural disasters such as wildfires.

We can plan and prepare for a potential natural disaster if we take the time to work with others to find ways of reducing damage and improve safety. Learning from past disasters provides information about how to improve our response time and behavior when future wildfires occur.

2015 was the largest wildfire season in the history of the United States. More than **10 MILLION ACRES** (4 million ha) of land burned.

A spark can be caused by a number of things: discarded cigarettes, downed power lines, a lightning strike, or embers from a campfire.

Destructive Forces

Wildfires occur all over the world. According to statistics, Portugal and Russia have the most wildfires in Europe. Portugal's fires are sparked by dry, hot summers and poor management of forest lands. Russia's fires, in the Siberian forests, were allowed to burn every summer for years because the government felt they were too costly to fight. Every year in the United States, 4–5 million acres (1.6-2 million ha) of land is destroyed by more than 100,000 wildfires. The western states are often hardest hit, including Montana, Idaho, Wyoming, Washington, Colorado, Oregon, and California. In these areas, wildfire causes are present most of the year, including frequent thunderstorms, **drought**, and dry, hot temperatures.

"ON EARTH, SOMETHING IS ALWAYS BURNING."
NASA's Earth Observatory

Wildfire zones are areas on a map indicating places in the world where wildfires have occurred often. In this map, the areas in orange and red show how the wildfire season lengthened from 1979 to 2014. Areas in yellow show where the wildfire season stayed the same.

CASE STUDY
Winds and the Witch Creek Fire

On October 21, 2007, the Santa Ana winds caused power lines to spark a fire near Witch Creek, California. These strong winds form when high pressure air from areas inland meet low pressure winds from the coast. In less than 24 hours, the winds caused the Witch Creek Fire to spread to the city limits of San Diego. In total, 1,125 homes were destroyed, 40 firefighters were injured battling the blaze, and two people were killed.

To learn from this event, scientists at the U.S. Forest Service (USFS) and the National Institute of Standards and Technology (NIST) collected **data** about the fire, its effects, and the outcomes for homeowners. They looked at the materials used to build homes and other structures, and they compared the levels of damage that resulted. This information was then used to create a **hazard scale** to predict the amount of damage that may occur to homes in the event of a future wildfire. By using data from an actual wildfire event, scientists were able to create a tool that measures wildfire risk. This tool can be used to make better choices about building materials to reduce the potential for damage and loss.

After the Witch Creek Fire, community improvements were made, including stricter building codes, new evacuation routes, and better emergency training for residents.

Studying the devastation caused by wildfires helps researchers determine ways to best avoid, fight, and recover from them.

CHAPTER 1

The Science Behind Wildfires

Wildfires can be dangerous and damaging to property, but they actually have a role to play in the ecosystem. Wildfires that occur naturally are nature's way of maintaining order in the environment. Some wildfires cause a positive change through the destruction of dead or diseased vegetation, and the removal of harmful insects or **invasive species**.

Controlled Burns

To encourage this removal and regrowth, firefighters sometimes use a controlled burn to imitate the behavior of a wildfire. These are fires deliberately set to reduce the risk of larger, more destructive wildfires. They are also called prescribed burns or hazard reduction burns. Another way wildfires can benefit the vegetation in a forest is by allowing more sunlight to filter through what was previously thick tree cover and undergrowth, so seeds can take root and grow. When wildfires burn **fuel sources** such as trees and other vegetation, nutrients are released into the soil. This nutrient-rich soil allows the forest to go through **regeneration**, with new, healthy plants and trees.

These images show forest regeneration after a fire.

Fuel and Fire

A wildfire needs three elements to ignite and burn: fuel, oxygen, and a source of heat. This is commonly referred to as the "fire triangle." If one of these elements is missing, a fire will die out. Hot weather, wind, and dry vegetation together create an environment in which a wildfire can destroy large areas of land and forests within minutes. When these conditions are present, a spark is all that's needed to start a wildfire. As long as there is fuel and the right conditions for it to burn, the fire may last hours, days, weeks, or even months. The more fuel available, the more intense the wildfire. This is known as the fuel load, and includes grasses, trees, brush, and even homes.

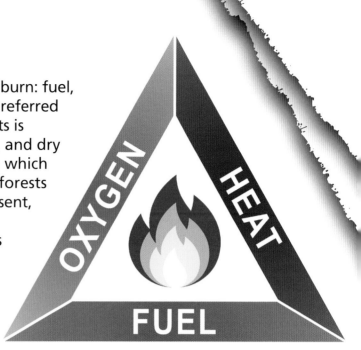

Types of Wildfires

Surface

Burning leaf litter and other vegetation close to the ground, this fire causes the least amount of damage and is the easiest to put out. It also thins out the forest, making room for new growth.

Crown

The most dangerous type of wildfire and the most destructive, this fire burns from the base of trees all the way up to the top, or crown. Embers blown from these fires can travel quickly, spreading the wildfire to other locations.

Smoldering

This type of fire burns slowly and sometimes underground. It can last a long time and can be hard to control.

Wildland-Urban Interface

As wildfires move closer to urban areas, they approach the wildland-urban interface, or WUI. The WUI is where the forest, or rural, uninhabited land meets human development such as towns or cities. Fires that travel from wildland areas to human development are very dangerous, and people who live in the WUI are at the greatest risk of disaster during wildfires.

It Matters

Wildfires are dangerous, not only because they can reach urban areas and destroy homes, but also due to the fact that the burning material produces harmful smoke and pollutes the air with **particulate matter**. Particulate matter, or PM, is a combination of liquid droplets mixed with tiny particles in the air. This is harmful to people when they inhale it, potentially causing severe health problems, including asthma attacks, lung diseases, and heart problems.

Approximately **45 MILLION HOMES** in the United States are in the wildland-urban interface.

A WUI fire threatens a home in California

Changing Times

Climate change has a significant impact on natural disasters such as wildfires. It can increase the possibility of drought and unstable weather, and affects the length of time fires burn. This has an overall effect on how often they occur and how severe wildfires can become. These events can burn for days, or even weeks at a time.

Areas that have experienced periods of drought are more likely to have wildfires.

SCIENCE BIO
Creating the WUI Hazard Scale

In 2012, two scientists in the United States developed the first risk-management tool for wildfires that spread to urban areas, known as the Wildland-Urban Interface (WUI) Hazard Scale. Alexander Maranghides of the NIST worked with William Mell of the USFS to create this potentially lifesaving tool.

The scale is based on damage that was caused by wildfires where undeveloped areas meet urban development. It is an assessment tool that is used to determine better building codes and materials to provide the best protection for people and their property in communities that are at risk due to flames or embers. Each area in the WUI is examined, and a risk-level zone is assigned.

Residents in high-risk zones have specific building codes, material requirements, and landscaping expectations because they have a greater likelihood of exposure to wildfire and embers. This includes the use of materials that are **low combustible**, or difficult to ignite, **irrigation** systems for vegetation, and protective coverings that resist heat and fire damage. These precautions are now the standard in high-risk zones, based on the hazard scale.

E4

E3

Ravine

E2

E1

Peshtigo Wildfire

The Peshtigo Wildfire became the deadliest wildfire on record in the United States when more than 2,000 people were killed. It occurred in Wisconsin in fall 1871, after an unusually dry summer. It is believed that a number of fires that were meant to clear the land for farming sparked this fire. A combination of swirling winds, blowing embers, and fuel from brush and grasslands, caused several small fires to combine, developing into one massive, fast-moving wildfire.

As the temperature began to rise, winds blew harder, eventually creating a firestorm that consumed everything in its path, especially the homes and businesses which were almost entirely constructed from wood. Twelve prairie towns were destroyed, and more than 1.2 million acres (486,000 hectares) of land burned.

Making Changes

After the Peshtigo Wildfire, people looked for ways to help prevent future disasters. They realized their behaviors may have contributed to the fire. Logging practices, such as clearing the land and discarding unwanted timber and vegetation provided fuel for the fire. People realized that things needed to change, and awareness increased as a result of this disaster. Regulations for better land-clearing and disposal practices were eventually put in place.

*The Peshtigo Wildfire's fuel load (grasses, trees, structures), combined with extreme wind and high temperatures, created a firestorm that had **catastrophic** results.*

In strong winds, power lines sometimes blow against each other, causing electricity to arc, or jump, often starting a fire. Overloads during heavy use can also cause arcing.

Cause and Effect

Discovering what causes natural disasters is extremely important for moving forward and improving future outcomes but investigating causes of fires can take months. Investigators look for clues in things that were affected by fire, but not completely destroyed. They sometimes examine the way trees have been burned, which can tell them which direction the fire spread. They also analyze the temperature, weather patterns, wind, and soil conditions using data that was collected on the day the wildfire started.

Power Line Sparked

When investigators determined that 17 of Northern California's major fires in 2017 were sparked by power lines, the **utility company** in that region promised to shut off the power in certain weather conditions as a way to limit the possibility of starting a wildfire. With today's technology, meteorologists are better able to predict weather and identify conditions that cause wildfires than they were in the past. This gives people more warning and response time during wildfires.

Fire Breeds Fire

The weather plays a significant role in wildfires, often creating conditions that ignite or expand them. However, sometimes it is the fire itself that creates the weather conditions. The heat and smoke from extreme wildfires can be so intense that it causes hot air to rise rapidly, creating **pyrocumulus clouds**, or fire clouds. These are rare clouds that have the potential to create thunderstorms and sometimes even tornadoes. The lightning during these storms can strike and ignite more wildfires in new locations. They can also affect the wind, causing powerful gusts to blow burning embers toward new fuel sources, or blow down power lines, sparking new fires.

PYROCUMULUS CLOUDS

can produce dry lightning, or lightning without rain, igniting wildfires in places where the fire conditions are perfect.

The average length of the North American wildfire season is now **20 PERCENT LONGER** *than it was 35 years ago.*

Rain and Humidity

In many cases, wildfires combust where vegetation has had time to dry out, often during periods of little or infrequent rainfall. Traditionally, it was thought that a downpour of rain would stop a wildfire through the soaking of trees, grass, and brush. Researchers have discovered that the **humidity level** during periods of rain is what helps to slow down the progress of a wildfire more than the actual rain itself. The humidity cuts through the dry air conditions that encourage combustion.

Often, the roots and inside of the trees burn, and a sudden downpour of rain will not reach far enough to put the fire out. The amount of rain isn't as critical as the length of time that it rains. A drizzle, or light rain, that lasts all day has a better chance of affecting the spread of a wildfire than a sudden downpour that lasts only a short time. Consistently falling rain seeps into the soil and plant debris on the forest floor, but a downpour runs off and doesn't soak into the fuel sources.

Slowing Down the Fire

Even though firefighters sometimes use aerial firefighting techniques such as water bombing, these techniques only serve to slow down a fire by wetting the fuel sources, not extinguishing it completely. It would be difficult to transport and drop enough water to put out a wildfire, but by slowing it down, firefighters have a better chance of controlling it.

Safety First

Scientists are actively working on ways to make people safer by developing technologies to help predict, and even prevent, wildfires in the future. Their data has revealed that over the last 35 years in North America, the approximate area burned by wildfires has doubled. New discoveries about the behavior of wildfires give us clues about how to improve our response to the wildfires of tomorrow.

CHAPTER 2

Studying Wildfires and Their Effects

Incident meteorologists take measurements of wildfires and gather data from the GOES 17 satellite.

Discovering details about wildfire behavior is difficult, because until recently, most information was gathered *after* a wildfire, instead of during the event. Today, researchers known as incident meteorologists are able to receive real-time updates from weather satellites. They also travel to the perimeter of wildfires to use measurement tools to determine wind speeds, temperature, and humidity levels. Equipped with radios, incident meteorologists communicate directly with firefighters to update them on weather patterns that may have negative or positive effects on the fires they are battling.

GOES 17

One of the weather satellites that researchers get current information from is the Geostationary Operational Environmental Satellite called GOES 17. It orbits Earth, monitoring clouds, storms, moisture, rainfall, and even fires or hotspots on Earth's surface. Forecasters use this data to locate possible wildfires, or predict areas that are likely to develop wildfires.

The GOES East and GOES West satellites captured this image showing wildfires spreading across Alaska and Canada in July 2019. The wildfires released an estimated 100 megatons of carbon dioxide (CO_2) into the atmosphere over two months. CO_2 contributes to climate change.

Climate Change and Fires

With warmer temperatures and changes to weather patterns due to climate change, even countries in the far north near the Arctic Circle are experiencing severe wildfires. In 2018, during the hottest July on record in Sweden, wildfires destroyed more than 61,000 acres (24,686 ha) of land. For several weeks, most of the country experienced temperatures higher than 86 degrees Fahrenheit (30 °C). At the same time, they were experiencing extreme drought.

While it isn't unusual for some wildfires to occur in Sweden, the size and amount of damage during that summer was significant. Lack of rain, intense heat, and windy conditions created uncontrollable fires. Help was called in from other countries, including Norway, Germany, France, Italy, Denmark, and Poland. Some aircraft were used to water bomb the fires, dousing some of the flames so firefighters could get closer. The Swedish Civil Contingencies Agency called it the country's "most serious wildfire situation of modern times."

Investigators believe that the wildfires in Sweden in summer 2018 were started by discarded disposable barbecues, even though there was a ban on any open-air fires at the time.

July 2019

Lena River

In 2019, fires in the **KRASNOYARSK** *region of Siberia in Russia consumed an area* **LARGER THAN THE COUNTRY OF GREECE** *in 8 months.*

Fires burn each year in the forests of Siberia in Russia. Climate change is contributing to larger fires that burn for longer.

150 km

CASE STUDY
Paradise Lost

The town of Paradise, California, in the Sierra Nevada foothills, suffered the state's deadliest wildfire on record in November 2018. There had been wildfires in that area before, but none were as fast-moving, as destructive, or as deadly as the Camp Fire. This fire was named after Camp Creek Road where the first spark ignited. Early in the morning, power company Pacific Gas and Electric (PG&E) detected a **power outage** on one of their lines along Camp Creek Road. This was about 10 miles (16 km) from Paradise. The damage to one of the utility's towers and downed power lines are considered the most likely cause of the fire.

Dry and Hot

The fire started during a dry, hot day with low humidity and very strong winds. Some areas had experienced no significant rain for more than 200 days. The location of the town on a ridge between two canyons made it impossible to evacuate everyone by car since there was only one main highway out of town. Evacuation plans that had been in place did not account for how fast the fire traveled, or the fact that blowing embers created **spot fires** on all sides of the town, forcing everyone to evacuate at the same time. The fire traveled a football-field length every minute, leaving people with little or no time to escape. More than 80 people died, some trapped in vehicles as they tried to flee. Ninety percent of Paradise was destroyed, including 14,000 homes.

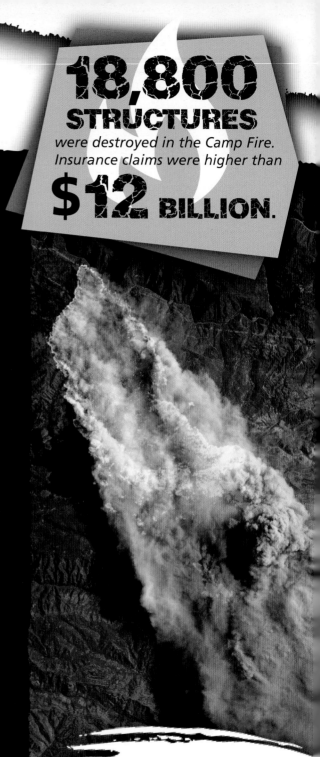

A malfunction in an electrical line caused the deadly Camp Fire. This prompted new rules for electricity providers in California. Repairs to old or faulty equipment and careful clearing of fuel sources near power lines are now standard safety practices to reduce the risk of wildfires.

Rebuilding for a Better Future

Paradise began rebuilding soon after the wildfire. They decided to make some important changes for the future. Researchers collected data about the objects that were burned and used those as indicators for analyzing the fire and making recommendations. Building materials must include fire-resistant protection, and forests that naturally regenerate will be thinned to prevent the overgrowth of trees. Other vegetation will be monitored, and regulations will be put in place to prevent the overgrowth of a fuel source.

The city of Rancho Palos Verdes, California, has 300 goats feed on conservation land each spring to prevent the overgrowth of wildfire fuel such as weeds and brush.

The Greenhouse Effect

Wildfires release gases as they burn. Carbon dioxide and carbon monoxide are two gases that have an effect on the environment after a wildfire. Researchers from the University of California, Berkeley, found that wildfires in that state created about 69 million tons (63 million metric tons) of carbon between 2001 and 2010. These emissions cause the atmosphere to experience more warming, which in turn affects the climate and creates more hot, dry seasons which are perfect conditions for wildfires to occur.

Forest Destruction

Wildfires that destroy forests affect the removal of carbon dioxide from our environment since Earth's natural air cleaners are trees. As the regrowth of forests takes place, eventually some of that carbon dioxide will be absorbed by the trees again. This creates a cycle, with climate change affecting the frequency and combustion of wildfires, and the wildfires then affecting climate change.

339,000 PEOPLE

worldwide died each year from 1997 to 2006, due to the effects of wildfire smoke.

During one week in October 2017, 250 wildfires devastated California's wine country region, emitting as much carbon dioxide as all of the cars and trucks produced in the state that year. NASA's Advanced Spaceborne Thermal Emission and Reflection Radiometer (ASTER) on its Terra satellite took this image showing vegetation in red, active fires in yellow, and smoke above wine country in blue-gray.

Firefighters who battle wildfires frequently show signs of decreased lung function for a period of time after the blaze.

Wildfires and Health

In addition to the dangers of damage to homes and the risk of death, wildfires can have a negative effect on health. Hundreds of harmful chemicals are contained within the smoke from wildfires. As that smoke drifts into the atmosphere, it deposits those chemicals in the form of gases, liquids, and solids that people may inhale or ingest. Particulate matter remains in the air, polluting it long after the fire.

More at Risk

Soil can store these harmful chemicals too. These chemicals have a negative effect on living things, causing eye irritation, breathing difficulties, throat soreness, headaches, nausea, dizziness, heart conditions, and possibly serious disease. With an increase in wildfires in many countries around the globe, more and more people may be at risk of developing health issues resulting from the **pollutants** wildfires produce.

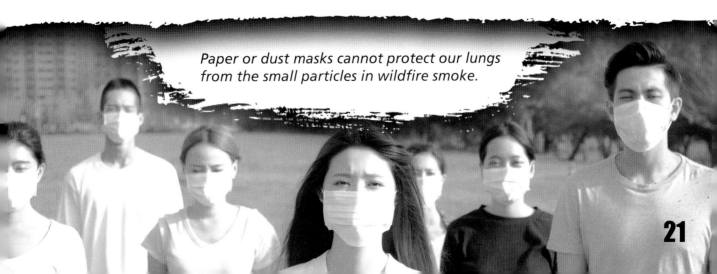

Paper or dust masks cannot protect our lungs from the small particles in wildfire smoke.

21

CHAPTER 3

Meeting the Challenge

Long-term prevention is necessary to combat wildfires and the damage they do. Communities must work together to find ways of reducing the risk and increasing the survival rates when wildfires occur. Technology, research, and innovative building materials are some of the ways people are reducing the hazards of wildfires around the world.

Fighting Chance

Many countries that often experience wildfires have developed fire response systems and emergency crews to respond to different kinds of wildfires in effective ways. Researchers have analyzed data about wildfires over time, and this data has helped firefighters to understand and respond to wildfires before they get out of control.

Initial Attack

An "initial attack" refers to early detection and immediate response by a crew of three or more firefighters who are the first ones at the scene of a wildfire. With this small first-response crew, initial-attack fires are often controlled within several hours. They work close to the fire for short periods of time. If a wildfire grows out of control before the initial-attack fire crew can control it, more help is called in, and the fire is upgraded to a **project wildfire**. It can take days, or months to fight project wildfires.

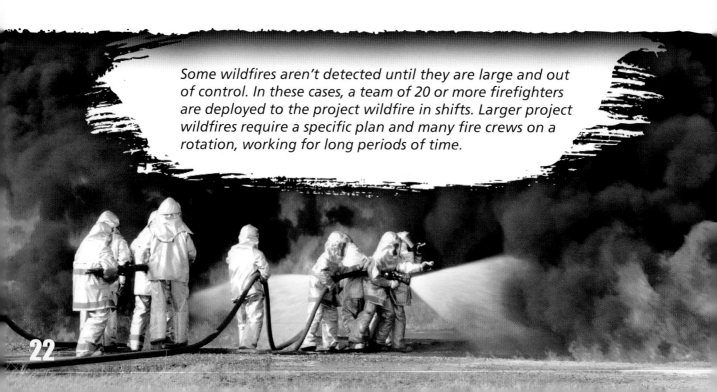

Some wildfires aren't detected until they are large and out of control. In these cases, a team of 20 or more firefighters are deployed to the project wildfire in shifts. Larger project wildfires require a specific plan and many fire crews on a rotation, working for long periods of time.

Controlled, or prescribed, burns require skill and planning. Most are set in spring or late fall.

Controlling Wildfires

Firefighters use what are called **suppression techniques** for fighting fires. These can include trenches, **firebreaks**, and water bombing. Digging trenches around the perimeter of a fire creates a firebreak by clearing the fuel source, such as vegetation, ahead of a fire. The firebreak is intended to prevent spreading. Fire crews also drop water and chemical fire retardants from the air to try to extinguish the fire. Controlled burns are used before a fire spreads. In this, firefighters deliberately burn the dry underbrush that could otherwise provide fuel to the larger fire.

Firestarting History

Controlled burns have been practiced by Indigenous peoples for thousands of years. People called firekeepers set fires to clear brush, renew growth, and make natural fireguards. The practice was discouraged by non-Indigenous governments that didn't have the same knowledge of the land and emphasized fire suppression instead. More recently, scientists say the practices of firekeepers burning small areas kept huge, intense fires from starting. Researchers in British Columbia, Canada, found historical evidence that **boreal forests** were burned to the ground in patchwork patterns every 75 to 100 years. As they learned forests have to be burned to grow healthy, governments turned to the traditional knowledge of firekeepers and controlled burns.

23

Early Detection

Scientists are attempting to improve the forecasting and detection of wildfires by using modern technology and computer **models**. These are designed to show how environmental conditions affect how wildfires begin and how long they last. It is not easy to detect naturally ignited wildfires early when they result from lightning strikes.

Even though weather satellites can reveal when and where lightning storms are happening, not every strike ignites a fire. Some areas where wildfires are more common have lightning **sensors** that show accurate information about the location of lightning strikes. However, since lightning strikes happen often, it is not possible to go out and check the site of each strike to see if a wildfire was ignited. Because of this, many wildfires grow out of control, undetected for a period of time.

Tracking Wildfires

The Suomi NPP weather satellite allows researchers for the National Oceanic and Atmospheric Administration (NOAA) to see Earth's surface through high-resolution **infrared images**. The satellite uses a sensor known as the VIIRS (Visible Infrared Imaging Radiometer Suite). It can detect wildfires in remote locations that would otherwise be undetected until out of control.

Lightning reduced this tree to a hollowed-out glowing trunk. The fire here was contained to just one tree, but many lightning strikes result in major fires.

Suomi NPP

Computer Modeling

The sensor sends detailed data about active wildfires, which is then transferred to a computer model. The model takes the VIIRS data and builds an accurate outline of where a fire is burning, how widespread it is, and how intense it is. This information gives forestry management teams and firefighters details they may not be able to discover on land.

Sending Alerts

Technology such as the VIIRS allows fire-management teams to send out early alerts when a wildfire is detected. This technology also works at night, so researchers are able to track patterns at any time of day, receiving data that can potentially save lives. Because satellites orbit Earth once every 12 hours, data is relayed by VIIRS in near-real time, making it easier to get information in a timely way to ground crews fighting fires.

Models give forestry teams a valuable tool for predicting wildfire behavior with more detail and accuracy. Preparation is key to effectively fighting wildfires.

[fire counts per year per grid cell]

Boreal Forest Fire

The Fort McMurray Wildfire was a catastrophic natural disaster that took place in May 2016 in Alberta, Canada. It is the largest wildfire Alberta has ever experienced. Dense boreal forest surrounds the northern community of Fort McMurray, placing the town in the wildland-urban interface.

Flammable Materials

Trees in boreal forests normally have low moisture and high **resin** content, making them very dry and flammable. The fire is believed to have been started by humans, as lightning was ruled out as a cause. It quickly spread to the nearby town of Fort McMurray. The weather conditions at the time were hot and dry, with strong winds. More than 80,000 people were evacuated from their homes, and more than 2,400 buildings were completely destroyed. Due to a plan for effective evacuation procedures, and the efforts of the Red Cross, almost everyone made it out of the danger zone safely. Sadly, two young people lost their lives in a traffic accident on the evacuation route.

More than 1,700 firefighters came to Fort McMurray to help battle the raging wildfires.

Fires burn an average of **56,834,237 ACRES** *(23 million ha)* of land across Canada each year. That **DOUBLED IN 2015.**

More than **24,710 ACRES** *(10,000 ha) and* **1,600 STRUCTURES** *were destroyed in the Fort McMurray Wildfire.*

SCIENCE BIO
Alan Westhaver and the Institute for Catastrophic Loss Reduction

In the days and weeks that followed the Fort McMurray Wildfire, researchers analyzed what happened to the town. They were particularly interested in why so many homes and businesses in Fort McMurray's WUI were damaged or destroyed, yet many others were not. Alan Westhaver, a researcher who produced a report for the Institute for Catastrophic Loss Reduction in London, Ontario, Canada, studied homes that were spared. He compared them with homes that were destroyed or badly damaged.

Westhaver's findings led him to conclude that it was embers blown by strong winds over long distances that damaged the homes, and not direct contact with flames. He discovered that homes where fuel sources were available, such as leaf litter, shrubs, building materials, decks, and wood piles, were more likely to have been ignited by flying hot embers. This caused more ignition in the neighborhoods, allowing the fire to spread through the town. In contrast, several homes that did not have many of these flammable items nearby were better able to avoid destruction.

Westhaver concluded that educating homeowners and the government about building materials and the plants they used in their yards and gardens would be the best way to reduce the impact of future wildfires on communities bordering wildlands. His research is helping people understand the behavior of wildfires and how to best protect homes from future wildland-urban interface fires.

Wildfires can produce millions of embers which ignite new spot fires wherever they land, often destroying homes.

3-D Wildfire Prediction

Some scientists have developed simulation technology called FIRETEC that uses a computer code to analyze what actually happens within a wildfire. This 3-D program displays information about the weather, combustion, air flow, and processes that occur inside the fire. It also shows how those factors can affect the spread, growth, or changes that happen. Developed by the Los Alamos National Laboratory in New Mexico, FIRETEC is a useful tool for predicting future wildfire behavior.

This model can determine how future wildfires are handled, as well as provide training opportunities for firefighters, and offer valuable information about fuel sources, combustion, and atmospheric conditions.

Time = 380

The unpredictable nature of wildfires makes simulation technology essential for discovering the best strategies for battling and suppressing them in the future.

Flames travel upward because heat energy warms the air above a fire. Every **10 DEGREE** increase in the angle of a hill or slope **DOUBLES A FIRE'S SPEED.**

Fires, especially large ones, force air upward. This creates a vacuum that usually pulls the air to the front of the wildfire, spreading it forward. Sometimes, the fire changes direction, responding to the force of the air in unexpected ways.

Many things can become fuel sources in a wildfire, including wooden fences or sheds located close to homes.

Fire Prevention Measures

Wildfires are not always preventable, but the loss of property and loss of life can be. People who live in the WUI have a responsibility to themselves and others to become educated about the fire protection behaviors that will help create safer structures and living spaces. They must work together with government and local fire protection services to put fire prevention procedures in place, and to follow recommended practices.

Eliminating Fire Fuel

To reduce the damage to homes and property, homeowners must eliminate potential fuel sources around their living spaces, moving all combustible materials such as firewood and outdoor furniture a safe distance from the home. Embers and firebrands (pieces of burning bark, branches, or pinecones) travel from the wildfire on the strong winds, often landing on homeowners' properties.

Spot Fires

Most of the time, embers die out and don't ignite materials, but in some cases, spot fires result from an ember or firebrand. Gardens with mulch, dry grasses, shrubs, decks, and roofs are potentially flammable materials that, once ignited, can spread fire to surrounding buildings. Keeping leaf litter and debris out of yards and gutters, and using landscaping materials and vegetation that are considered "low-risk," are some ways homeowners can help prevent damage during a wildfire.

Proactive Protection

Taking steps to protect the public from the threat of wildfire has been a goal of many government programs in countries around the world. An awareness program that the U.S. Forest Service started during World War II in 1944, warned people of the dangers of wildfires through a national advertising system. Originally, the program was designed to bring awareness to possible enemy shelling attacks on California's coast.

Smokey Bear

Fearing that further attacks might set off large-scale wildfires, they came up with a plan to inform the public. Smokey Bear became the mascot for posters, billboards, and eventually television commercials. The U.S. Forest Service believed that if they used a cartoon bear dressed as a forest ranger, people would take more interest in safety and fire prevention. The idea worked. Smokey Bear has been a symbol of fire prevention and education for more than 75 years. That's the longest-running public service advertising program in United States history.

Human-Caused Bush Fires

In Australia, 80 percent of bush fires are human-caused. A high percentage of these are from arson. In response to this, researchers and community groups are working together to lower the risks and frequency of these fires through awareness about human involvement, and crime reporting and prevention.

Eliminating Threats

Being proactive, or taking action to cause change rather than reacting to a change, can save lives. In Colorado, the White Mountain Stewardship's fuel treatment plan helped prevent a wildfire from destroying more than 1,400 homes. Strong winds and dry air caused a wildfire to spread to the WUI in the community of Silverthorne in June 2018. As it traveled through the crowns of the trees, it spread rapidly until it was forced to drop to ground level due to a sudden lack of trees.

Fuelbreak

The gap was a human-made fuelbreak that had been carefully cleared out to leave a 0.5 mile (0.8 km) separation between the forest and the homes in the WUI. The fuelbreak dramatically slowed the spread of the fire, giving people time to react. This proactive treatment, combined with careful fuel prevention practices among homeowners, helped stop the fire from spreading to nearby houses.

Firefighters were able to fight the fire on the ground and from the air, effectively protecting the properties and homes that otherwise would have been in the fire's path. By working together, residents and fire protection services were able to prevent a potential disaster from happening in their community.

Fuelbreaks help prevent the spread of wildfires to homes in the wildland-urban interface.

CASE STUDY
Paradise's Practice Drills

Some communities have developed wildfire evacuation plans to allow residents to leave safely and quickly. But surprisingly, many communities that often have wildfires do not have any established evacuation strategies. In California, communities are not required to have official evacuation plans.

Prepared but Not Prepared

Paradise did have an evacuation plan when the 2018 Camp Fire occurred, and residents regularly participated in practice drills. Each year, every resident in Paradise received a copy of the evacuation plan in the mail. However, when the deadly wildfire threatened the town, Paradise wasn't as prepared as they thought. They didn't have a plan for evacuating the entire town all at once.

In the past, fires entered the town from one direction, allowing time to evacuate specific areas of the town at a time. But the Camp Fire was different. Embers rained down on the town from all sides, and the fire moved faster than anyone predicted. The result was disastrous. Three out of the five roads leading out of town were closed because the fire had come too close. The other two roads were then overloaded and clogged, and people panicked. Some cars ran out of gas, and many people simply left their cars in the middle of the road and fled on foot, blocking the route. Others remained as the fire surrounded them. At least eight people died inside vehicles on the evacuation route.

Future Plans

After the fire, emergency leaders in Paradise determined that the disaster would have been worse if the town had not conducted drills. The goals for the future are to set evacuation plans in place as though all fires were ember fires.

fire embers

Winds pushed the Camp Fire into Paradise quickly. On the morning of the fire, three of the town's 14 zones received warnings, but not mandatory evacuation orders. Some experts say that the unpredictability of wildfires makes it difficult to fully prepare an effective evacuation plan.

Recovery for Wildlands

Fires are natural and often necessary for forests to remain healthy, but the extreme wildfires that have occurred recently around the world are threatening to destroy more than just dead or diseased vegetation. Severe wildfires are burning so hot that all parts of the ecosystem are affected, including the soil, which becomes scorched, making it non-absorbent. When this happens, seeds that normally grow in nutrient-rich soil fail to take root. Water becomes runoff when it can't be absorbed, potentially flooding nearby communities.

Harming Regeneration

Natural forest regeneration can't take place when the land is too burned or swamped with water. This affects plant growth, animal habitat renewal, and human health and safety. Eventually, hardy shrubs will grow, but trees won't. Experts warn that when this happens, vast shrublands will replace forests, which in turn will fuel future wildfires.

Helping Recovery

One way people are helping forest recovery is by physically removing unstable dead and dying vegetation and trees. It helps the forest to recover more quickly, encouraging regrowth, and protecting landowners from the threat of falling trees and limbs after the fire. To plant seeds and ensure water can be absorbed, the soil is often tilled by volunteers. By taking care of forests and property after wildfires, residents living in the wildland-urban interface are helping the environment recover after devastation.

Burn scars are areas of land where all the vegetation has been burned. They can lead to other disasters, such as flash floods, because the land cannot absorb a lot of water.

What was once forest is now brush and shrubs, providing a combustible fuel source for wildfires.

Debris from burned-out properties is removed in preparation for rebuilding.

Recovery for Communities

To return to urban communities that have suffered from wildfire damage, many government and local authorities must agree that it is safe to do so. Water, sewer, gas, and hydroelectric services must be restored. To rebuild structures such as homes and businesses that have been destroyed, insurance companies assess the damage to calculate what is needed to fund the repairs or construction costs. Sometimes, local and federal government agencies provide funds to assist people with the high costs of development.

Finding Help

Websites and Internet apps can be helpful tools for organizing relief and rebuilding efforts in communities that have suffered natural disasters such as hurricanes, tornadoes, or wildfires. The website www.recovers.org is a free site designed to create opportunities for volunteers to assist those in need, and for people to seek out help with recovery. It provides information, connects residents with local government agencies, and allows volunteer organizations to pinpoint areas of need in the community.

The charity Habitat for Humanity rebuilt 20 homes destroyed by wildfires on an Indigenous reservation in Valley Center, California.

CHAPTER 4

Facing Future Disasters

Since the middle of the 1980s, wildfires have increased in number and duration, as well as severity. As Earth's climate gets warmer, it affects moisture levels and precipitation. When soil dries out, and precipitation levels change, drought sets in, making conditions perfect for a random lightning strike, or human error to ignite a wildfire. Hot, dry conditions are spawning more intense, longer-lasting wildfires. The economy suffers when infrastructure, communities, and the environment are damaged because rebuilding and recovery efforts cost a lot of time and money.

A technician uses a computer to follow the flight pattern of an uncrewed aerial vehicle, or drone, that helps firefighters detect, map, and contain fires.

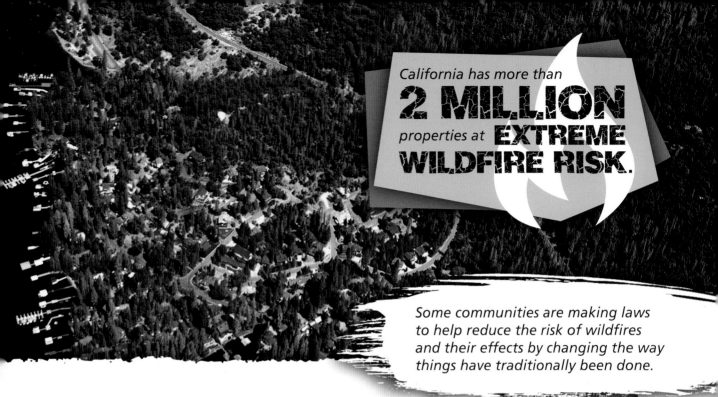

California has more than **2 MILLION** properties at **EXTREME WILDFIRE RISK.**

Some communities are making laws to help reduce the risk of wildfires and their effects by changing the way things have traditionally been done.

Changing the Way Things Are Done

Studying past wildfire disasters has led to new discoveries about the way things have been done, and why changes are necessary to reduce the risks for people in WUI areas.

Electric power lines have traditionally been strung overhead from tall wooden poles. This has had an effect on wildfires, because many have been ignited when high winds have snapped the lines or knocked trees across them. When researchers considered ways to make electricity delivery safer, they realized that burying the electrical lines underground would reduce power-line-ignited wildfires. An additional benefit to "**undergrounding**" the lines was that no poles or downed wires would affect potential evacuation routes.

Undergrounding

As a result of this research, many communities in high-risk wildfire zones are currently requiring undergrounding in new housing developments and urban construction. In California, the third leading cause of wildfires is damaged electrical equipment and power lines. Undergrounding is one way to reduce the wildfire risk.

Using Drones

Technologies that can monitor from the air provide information about destructive wildfires. Drones are small, uncrewed aircraft that are equipped with cameras. The location and threat level of the wildfire is communicated through alerts to firefighters on the ground and in the air. Drones also have the ability to track wildfires at night, in areas where bigger aircraft may not be able to reach. By mapping the fire and indicating where hotspots are, drones are helping fire crews and evacuation efforts with timely, accurate information.

Drones with infrared cameras can track a fire from a safe distance.

SCIENCE BIO
Lockheed Martin's K-MAX

In 2015, Lockheed Martin, an American aerospace and global engineering company, tested its remote-controlled full-size helicopter as a firefighting machine. Originally developed to carry heavy cargo deliveries to American marines during the war in Afghanistan, the K-MAX helicopter was able to travel to specific, remote locations without a human pilot.

When the helicopter successfully made those deliveries, the company looked for other ways it could be useful. Fighting wildfires was a natural fit.

The helicopter was moved into position, following behind a smaller fire-scouting drone called the Indago. The K-MAX was successful in dropping enough fire-retardant to extinguish a staged fire. In another test, the K-MAX was able to carry and drop more than 12 tons (10,900 kg) of water in one hour on a specific target. This technology has lifesaving potential, not only because it can fight wildfires in all conditions, day or night, but also because it has the ability to protect the lives of firefighters and pilots during wildfire events.

Firefighting Robots

The extreme heat of today's wildfires prevents firefighters from getting close, making it difficult to extinguish the flames. Scientists have developed a way to combat this through the use of specially designed robots that can enter fire zones too hot for humans to access. Some robots have hose attachments, others have built-in water tanks. Equipped with cameras, these robots have the ability to send detailed information back to the human firefighters, offering a view of the wildfire that otherwise would never be seen.

The Thermite robot (above) was developed by Howe and Howe Technologies in Maine. It is remote-controlled, and is connected to a water source through a hose. Its small size allows it to access small spaces.

The TAF35 (Turbine Aided Firefighting robot, right) is able to spray water up to 295 feet (90 m). It was developed by engineers in Germany for use in a variety of firefighting events in New South Wales, Australia. It is also able to spray mist and foam, making it a versatile firefighting robot.

Machines Do the Work

Artificial intelligence (AI) is the ability of machines such as computers to be programmed to perform tasks by simulating human thinking. This technology allows machines to perform tasks that might be impossible or extremely dangerous for humans. AI is used in many applications around the world, including fighting wildfires.

AI and Wildfires

If firefighters could predict that a wildfire would spread into an area with a highly combustible fuel source such as shrubs and brush, they could plan their response effectively. The tools and number of firefighters could therefore match the urgency of the fire. A wildfire has a faster rate of spread in dry brush than it would in a less-combustible area, such as a well-watered golf course. Using AI information and predictions, firefighting services can use their teams more effectively. Several fire departments in California have started using predictive technology such as WIFIRE. Developed by the University of California, WIFIRE combines satellite images with information from hundreds of remote weather stations to predict the path of a wildfire.

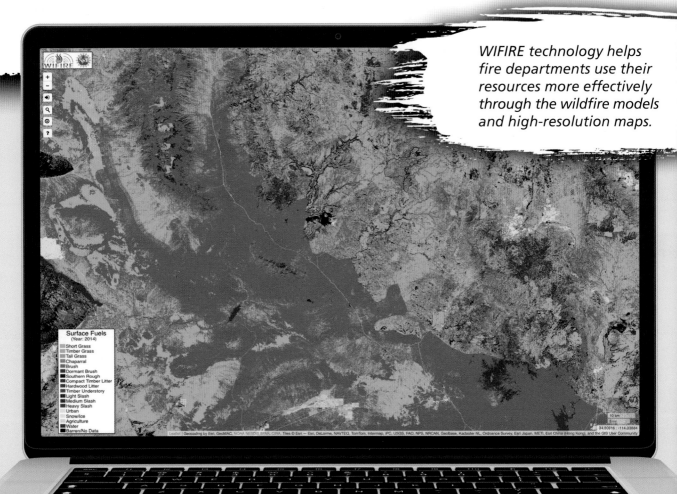

WIFIRE technology helps fire departments use their resources more effectively through the wildfire models and high-resolution maps.

Virtual Reality

Even with the help of AI, wildfires are unpredictable, ever-changing events that require human understanding and firefighting abilities. Training firefighters for real-life responses to wildfires is difficult. Recently, the U.S. Forest Service has introduced an innovative method for training a special group of firefighters known as smokejumpers. These firefighters use parachutes to go into hard-to-reach areas during a wildfire.

Simulating Fires

To confidently train the smokejumpers without sending them into actual wildfires, fire crews are using virtual reality (VR). Through the use of 3-D images, this simulation tool allows firefighters to train for a variety of possible situations that might occur during a wildfire. It provides a representation of possible events and conditions that trainers are able to control or change while the firefighters experience it through 3-D visual equipment. This training is safe and effective, preparing smokejumpers for any possible situation they may experience during a real wildfire event.

In a controlled environment, smokejumpers receive training through simulated experiences while watching a 3-D wildfire in VR.

41

CHAPTER 5

Fighting Future Fires

Wildfires are increasing in number. They are causing greater damage and destruction, and are lasting longer than ever before. Climate change is having an impact on wildfires across the globe, and by creating more CO_2, wildfires are affecting climate change in return.

Human activity and carelessness often cause wildfires. Weather patterns, such as storms, strong winds, and drought are becoming more severe due to climate change. These factors provide optimal conditions in high-risk areas for the "megafires" occurring today. Between 1986 and 2003, it was calculated that four times more wildfires occurred in the western United States than during the years between 1970 and 1986. The more recent fires were stronger, more destructive, and longer-lasting.

With today's technology, scientists are learning more about wildfires and the most proactive ways to prepare for, predict, and combat them. People living in wildland-urban interface regions are more informed than ever before, with many communities developing plans for wildfire safety. These include the use of nonflammable building materials, fire evacuation plans, practice drills, and early warning systems. Even though wildfires continue to threaten people's lives, innovative tools and advances in technology are reducing the loss of life and damage to property.

Some wildfires can change the landscape of an area, possibly triggering landslides or floods. When fire weakens the ecosystem of a forest or mountain landscape, additional natural disasters can occur.

Ask Yourself This

Based on the information in this book, what are some of the ways in which humans have learned from devastating wildfires and their aftereffects over the years?

1. Knowing that humans cause the majority of wildfires, think of some ways people can be prevention-minded and more careful in the future. What would the message be, and how would it reach people around the world so that wildfires decrease?

2. Fighting wildfires in the past looked different than it does today, thanks to innovative technologies. Can we use technology more effectively to fight wildfires? How will the development of new technologies have an impact on the future of wildfires?

3. Climate change is causing more extreme weather around the world. What can people do to reduce the risk of wildfire where they live? What are some ways to get more people involved with effective practices, such as clearing fuel sources and using low-combustible building materials?

43

Bibliography

Chapter 1

Averill, Clare. "Smoke from Siberian Taiga Fires." NASA Earth Observatory, October 9, 2003. https://go.nasa.gov/2mcs9bV

Ayres, Sabra. "Siberia just experienced wildfires on a staggering scale. Russia is rethinking how to fight them." *Los Angeles Times*, August 21, 2019. https://lat.ms/33Mpveg

"Fire." NASA Earth Observatory. https://go.nasa.gov/31NjKMr

Gould, Rod. "Lessons Learned From the Witch Creek Fire." *Western City*, October 1, 2008. https://bit.ly/2X0Zo3o

"Wildfire." Basic Planet, 2013. www.basicplanet.com/wildfire

Wolters, Claire. "Wildfires, Explained." *National Geographic*. https://on.natgeo.com/2GL3sfn

Chapter 2

"Elements of Fire." The Ad Council, 2019. https://bit.ly/2nATP5K

"Fire behaviour."Natural Resources Canada, June 21, 2019. https://bit.ly/2L5KCkK

"Fire Ecology & Management: Fire ignition, behavior & effects." Idaho Firewise, 2019. https://bit.ly/2RrtMy7

Havel, Gregory. "Remembering The Great Peshtigo Fire of 1871." Fire Engineering, October 8, 2007. https://bit.ly/2RD3J7j

Johnston, F.H., S.B. Henderson, Y. Chen, J.T. Randerson, M. Marlier, et al. "Estimated Global Mortality Attributable to Smoke from Landscape Fires." *Environmental Health Perspectives*, *120*(5), May 1, 2012. https://bit.ly/2l7jmI7

Maranghides, Alexander, and William Mell. "Framework for Addressing the National Wildland Urban Interface Fire Problem-Determining Fire and Ember Exposure Zones Using a WUI Hazard Scale." NIST, November 10, 2018. https://bit.ly/2XsBHQV

"Prescribed Fires." The Ad Council, 2019. https://bit.ly/2N1rZ0z

Radeloff, V.C., R.B. Hammer, S.I. Stewart, J.S. Fried, S.S. Holcomb, and J.F. McKeefry. "The Wildland-Urban Interface in the United States."

Ecological Applications, *15*(3), 799–805, June 1, 2005. https://doi.org/10.1890/04-1413

Sands, Yasmeen. "NIST and Forest Service Create World's First Hazard Scale for Wildland Fires." NIST, January 8, 2018. https://bit.ly/2IypfXz

Chapter 3

Daniels, Jeff. "Officials: Camp Fire, deadliest in California history, was caused by PG&E electrical transmission lines." *CNBC*, May 16, 2019. https://cnb.cx/2w0ciPm

Nyirady, Annamarie. "NOAA's GOES-17 Satellite is Now Operational." *Via Satellite*, February 13, 2019. https://bit.ly/2IYIDw5

Running, Steven W. "Is Global Warming Causing More, Larger Wildfires?" *Science, 313*, 927–928. August 18, 2006. https://fla.st/2IYcHYG

Watts, Jonathan. "Wildfires rage in Arctic Circle as Sweden calls for help." *The Guardian,* July 18, 2018. https://bit.ly/2Jy98H4

Chapter 4

Ahrens, Marty. "Lightning Fires and Lightning Strikes." National Fire Prevention Association, June 2013. https://bit.ly/2FYRCvD

Anderson, Dr. Kerry, Dr. Dan Thompson, and Brian Simpson. "FIRETEC—a Better Way to Understand Fire Behavior." *Insights,* Natural Resources Canada, 2016. https://bit.ly/2IZuUFf

Andone, Dakin. "It's not just spraying water: How the pros fight wildfires." *CNN*, December 9, 2017. https://cnn.it/2RqLO3i

Montgomery, Mike. "California Wildfire Season Is Coming. These New Technologies Could Help." *Forbes*, April 12, 2019. https://bit.ly/2J1NHjh

Schroeder, Wilfrid, Patricia Oliva, Louis Giglio, and Ivan A. Csiszar. "The New VIIRS 375 m active fire detection data product: Algorithm description and initial assessment." *Remote Sensing of Environment*, *143*, 85–96, December 17, 2013. https://bit.ly/2N52j6A

Westhaver, Alan. "Institute for Catastrophic Loss Reduction releases preliminary report into why some Fort McMurray homes survived in otherwise decimated neighbourhoods." *Cision*, August 22, 2016. https://bit.ly/2XnUugx

Learning More

Books

Garbe, Suzanne. *The Worst Wildfires of All Time*. Capstone Press, 2012.

Spilsbury, Louise, and Richard Spilsbury. *Wildfires*. Franklin Watts, 2017.

Thiessen, Mark. *Extreme Wildfires*. National Geographic Children's Books, 2016.

Websites

Check out this website for interactive graphics and more information about the way wildfires work. **https://go.nasa.gov/2QT7btf**

Find out more about ways to prevent wildfires in the future. **https://on.natgeo.com/2GL3sfn**

Learn about safety procedures around homes and in the outdoors to help prevent human-caused wildfires. **https://smokeybear.com**

Glossary

arson The act of setting fire to something on purpose

boreal forests Northern forests mostly made up of coniferous trees

catastrophic Devastating and life-changing

climate change Changing weather patterns over time, generally considered to be caused by human activity such as fossil fuel use

data Information

drought A long period of little or no rain, drying out all of the vegetation

firebreaks Cleared areas of land that prevent the spread of a wildfire to buildings nearby

fuel sources Anything that provides fuel, or a source for burning, such as grass, brush, shrubs, trees, or even homes

hazard scale A method of predicting the amount of damage that could happen to homes in the event of a wildfire

humidity level The amount of moisture present in the air

ignited Set on fire or caused to burn

infrared images Photos or images that show levels of heat

invasive species Animals or plants that are not normally found in a specific habitat

irrigation A controlled method for watering large areas of land or crops

low combustible Does not ignite, or catch fire easily

models Computer-generated representations based on data collected

particulate matter Very small bits of pollution in the air, made up of solids and liquids that can be toxic to breathe such as pollen, dust, smoke, or soot

pollutants Substances that contaminate or pollute air or water

power outage When the electricity source is damaged or shut off and no longer provides power for an extended time

project wildfire The name firefighters give to a wildfire that has grown out of control

pyrocumulus clouds Large, puffy clouds formed by heat and smoke from a wildfire and that can create lightning

regeneration Growing new plants and trees from seeds or roots after a fire

resin A very flammable sticky substance produced by some trees

rural Of or relating to the countryside

sensors Devices that can detect something specific and record data about it

spot fires Fires that occur when embers blow from the original wildfire, igniting new fires

suppression techniques Strategies that are used to try to suppress, or control, wildfires

undergrounding Burying power lines under the ground

urban Of or relating to a town or city

utility company A provider of services such as electricity or natural gas

Index

About the Author

Kylie Burns is an author and teacher who has always been fascinated by nature. Ever since she experienced a natural disaster when she was younger, she has been interested in finding out more about how they occur and why. She has written more than two dozen nonfiction books on a variety of topics, including animal life cycles, sports, famous celebrities, STEM science, and more.